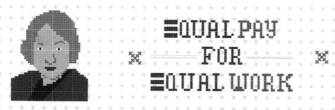

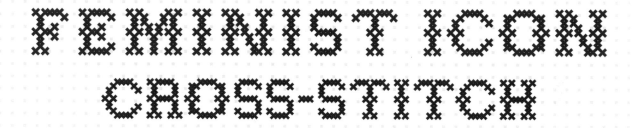

FEMINIST ICON CROSS-STITCH

By Anna Fleiss
and Lauren Mancuso

Running Press
PHILADELPHIA

Running Press
Hachette Book Group
1290 Avenue of the Americas, New York, NY 10104
www.runningpress.com
@Running_Press

Printed in China

First Edition: October 2017

Published by Running Press, an imprint of Perseus Books,
LLC, a subsidiary of Hachette Book Group, Inc.

The Hachette Speakers Bureau provides a wide range of authors for speaking events.
To find out more, go to www.hachettespeakersbureau.com or call (866) 376-6591.

The publisher is not responsible for websites (or their content) that are not owned by the publisher.

Stitching by Anna Fleiss, Alexandra Acosta, Sarah Mozal,
Nicole Paulhus, Bri LeRose, Evan Schmitt, and Brianne Richard

Photographs by Steve Legato

Print book cover and interior design by Amanda Richmond.

Library of Congress Control Number: 2017942104

ISBN: 978-0-7624-6290-2

LREX

10 9 8 7 6 5 4 3 2 1

Contents

Introduction ...4

Cross-Stitch Basics ...6

Patterns: The Women ...13

Cleopatra ...14

Queen Elizabeth I ...18

Abigail Adams ...22

Sojourner Truth ...26

Susan B. Anthony ...30

Marie Curie ...34

Virginia Woolf ...38

Eleanor Roosevelt ...42

Amelia Earhart ...46

Frida Kahlo ...50

Simone de Beauvoir ...54

Betty Friedan ...58

Ruth Bader Ginsburg ...62

Gloria Steinem ...66

Rosie the Riveter ...70

Billie Jean King ...74

Hillary Rodham Clinton ...78

Michelle Obama ...82

Beyoncé ...86

Malala Yousafzai ...90

Patterns: The Words ...95

Acknowledgments ...116

Index ...117

Introduction

Long before women were marching for the right to vote, they were cross-stitching. It was even part of the educational curriculum for the eighteenth-century girl. Young girls learned how to read, write, and grow into virtuous ladies through stitching their ABCs and moral verses in patterns called samplers. They proudly displayed their finished works on their walls. The samplers were a sign of female accomplishment, revealing both a lady's skills and her inner values. While the gentle craft of cross-stitch is still popular today, the values represented in modern patterns and how society views female accomplishment—or more aptly, accomplishment—have dramatically changed.

After all, a woman's place is no longer just in the home. It's in the Senate, the Supreme Court, the art room, and the laboratory. It's wherever she wants it to be. This book contains a collection of cross-stitch patterns for the modern-day feminist, warrior goddess, and rebel weirdo. The patterns depict twenty accomplished ladies to look up to and ten empowering verses to live by.

While these equally rad ladies may have lived at different times or in different places, they all have one thing in common: They show women that anything's possible. They have spoken out to improve education, expand women's rights, and revolutionize the way that women were defined by society altogether. From Queen Elizabeth I to Queen Bey, they have used their power to empower. They have slayed—whether in dominating in a male-dominated world or bringing more women into the feminist fold.

These women have broken the rules for what was and is right. Susan B. Anthony was arrested for voting in the 1872 presidential election. While the 19th Amendment wouldn't be ratified until 1920, Susan helped pave the way for the suffragettes that made it possible. Marie Curie took illegal classes at an underground university in Poland before heading off to the Sorbonne. The work that led to her two Nobel Prizes in physics and chemistry might not have happened if she didn't keep on keeping on. More recently, Malala Yousafzai took on the Taliban when they tried to stop young girls from going to school. Even after being shot on her school bus, Malala continues to fight for those denied the basic right to an education.

These heroes and pioneers have fought first-hand to make sure that women are treated equally. After Simone de Beauvoir pointed out in her intellectual musings that women were oppressed, Gloria Steinem and other second-wave feminists organized to fight against this oppression and expand women's rights. On the tennis court, Billie Jean King ensured that female athletes would be paid the same as their male counterparts. And even before Ruth Bader Ginsburg became notorious for her dissents, she was a lawyer on the other side of the bench arguing gender discrimination cases to ensure equal treatment for women on the job. These women have all helped make society a better place for everyone, and they have done it by going against the grain.

Similar to the cross-stitched samplers of yesteryear, these patterns of wall-worthy women and rousing sayings provide good starting points for your own inspiration. There are a lot of other heroes who belong on your wall right next to them—those the history books may have forgotten or those who haven't made history just yet.

Cross-Stitch Basics

WHAT IS CROSS-STITCH?

Before getting started, there are a few basics you should know about cross-stitch. The first is that cross-stitch is a particular style of embroidery, one in which you'll use a relatively dull needle—called a tapestry needle—to sew *x*-shaped stitches onto your fabric surface, creating a picture (in our case, of powerful ladies and rad sayings). Like other kinds of embroidery, cross-stitch can be done on a wide variety of fabrics, including clothes and linens (using a tool called waste cloth). In this book, though, we'll be working with a particular type of fabric, called Aida cloth, which is designed for cross-stitch.

SUPPLIES

One of the benefits of cross-stitch is how easy it is to get started—you'll only need a few tools to begin working. With cross-stitch fabric, tapestry needles, embroidery floss, a hoop, and some sharp scissors, you'll be whipping up portraits of your favorite feminists in no time.

Let's dig a little deeper into these tools.

FABRIC

Aida cloth is made specifically for cross-stitch projects. It is comprised of tiny squares so it is easy to see where each stitch belongs. Aida can be found at your local craft store or online. Pick up a bunch as cross-stitch can get addictive!

One thing to note about Aida cloth: each piece of cloth will have what's called a "count," also known as the number of squares per inch of fabric. For all of the patterns in this book, you'll want to use 11-count material—this has the fewest squares per inch and is the best fabric if you're new to cross-stitch. If you'd like to try more of a challenge, feel free to use a higher count (like 14- or 18-count); just know that the higher the count, the smaller your overall design will be once you're done.

To figure out the size of your pattern when you work in a different count of Aida cloth, simply divide the total number of stitches in your pattern (width) by the cloth's count (i.e. a pattern that is 66 stitches across on 14 cloth count is 4.74 inches wide).

NEEDLES AND THREAD

For any kind of embroidery project, you'll need a needle to pull your thread through the fabric. With cross-stitch, the best tool is a tapestry needle—the dull point on these needles will not snag or tear your fabric. Look for size 24 needles when you're gathering your supplies, and consider buying more than you think you'll need.

Thread is the most important, and the most fun, part of your cross-stitch arsenal. All of the patterns in this book use embroidery floss, which is a type of six-strand thread that is especially well-suited to cross-stitch. Each of the patterns will call for thread colors, noted by a DMC number; DMC is the most common brand of floss, and it offers a wide variety of shades. Once you've gotten the hang of cross-stitch, try switching out any of the pattern colors for your own favorites shades.

THE HARDWARE

When you're working on a cross-stitch project, the easiest way to keep your fabric steady is to use an embroidery hoop. These hoops can be made of wood or plastic, and they come in a range of sizes—pick the size that works best for your particular craft (most patterns in this book will need at minimum a six-inch hoop). Your hoop can be removed once you're done with your project, or you can finish you fabric right on the hoop and use it for display.

The more you cross-stitch, the more you'll learn that a pair of small scissors is your best friend. A pair of regular scissors will do in a pinch, but an extra-sharp pair will come in handy if you need to get into small areas or alter your work. Always be careful when using your embroidery scissors—you want to turn that sharpness on your fabric, not yourself.

METHOD

It's almost time to begin stitching! Cross-stitch is a very straightforward style of embroidery, since it's based around a single basic stitch that you repeat throughout the pattern. And using Aida cloth makes the process even simpler—the squares that comprise the cloth line up with where all of your stitches will be made.

Each of your stitches will be made up of two short strokes, called a top stitch and a bottom stitch. These stitches will cross diagonally, to create an X that fills the cloth square. In the patterns, you'll see these stitches noted by a solid square (with a color that corresponds to the thread you should be using). You'll occasionally see lines crossing on top of the patterns; these are called backstitches, and you'll use them to add some details to your patterns. We'll also use satin stitches to fill in the eyebrows in our patterns.

Before you begin stitching your feminist masterpiece, you'll need to get your fabric ready. To make sure you have enough room, plan on a piece of cloth that can accommodate your pattern, as well as a healthy border (usually a few inches on all sides). It's better to have a little too much fabric—which you can cut away later—than too little.

The last step is to thread your needle. Find the color that corresponds to the stitches that are in the center of your pattern (more on that in a moment), and cut a piece of thread that is roughly eighteen inches long. You'll then want to separate your piece of floss into strands. Each piece of embroidery floss is made up of six distinct strands, though you will only want to use three at a time when you're stitching. Typically, cross-stitch patterns use only two strands of floss. We'll be using three strands to achieve a denser, more saturated look.

STITCHING

First, find the center of your fabric—you don't need to be super precise, but try to get as close to the center as possible. This is where you'll want to begin stitching. Try folding your cloth in half both horizontally and vertically to find the center.

Your stitches will move from the center of the pattern outward. The patterns in this book use a method called "counted cross-stitch," meaning that you will base your stitches off of a pattern, rather than a design printed on the fabric. With this type of pattern, you'll count the number of stitches in the color you're using and then make those stitches on your fabric.

MAKING SINGLE CROSS-STITCHES

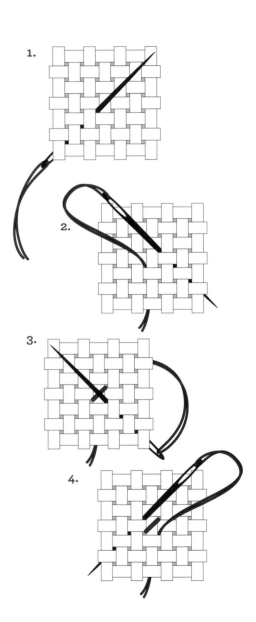

1. Once you've found the center of your fabric, you can begin making stitches. To start, you'll want to pull your thread up through the small hole at the bottom left corner of your starting square, being sure to leave a one-inch "tail" of floss on the underside of the fabric. Hold on to that tail as you make your next few stitches—you'll want the back side of your stitches to cover the tail, securing it in place instead of a lumpy knot.

2. Pull the rest of your thread up through the fabric and then sew through the top right corner of the same square, creating a diagonal stitch. You'll want to pull your thread through to the back of the fabric, taking care not to sew it too tightly— your goal should be a smooth surface, without any puckering from the floss. This is the first half of your stitch.

3. To create the second half of your stitch, sew up from the back of the fabric—through the bottom right corner of the square—to the front.

4. Pull your thread relatively taut, and then cross the square diagonally, sewing down through the top left hole. This will create the *x* shape of your cross-stitch.

5. Continue by making a stitch in the square next to your completed stitch. This square borders your first stitch, and shares two holes with it.

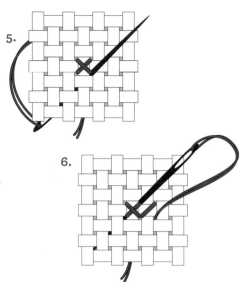

6. The stitches in each square should be made in the same direction, to keep your finished piece nice and even. Your first stitch will again be made from the bottom left to the top right; and then the bottom right to the top left.

MAKING MULTIPLE CROSS-STITCHES

Most of the time, you'll be creating rows of stitches in the same color, not just one isolated stitch. When you're looking to produce big blocks of color, you can use a handy shortcut to create horizontal rows.

1. You'll begin the same way you would for a single stitch—pull your needle up through the bottom left corner of your first square, and stitch across to the top right corner. Instead of finishing off that stitch, begin another half-stitch in the next square, again moving from the bottom left corner to the top right. Repeat this method until you've gone the full width of the section you're working on.

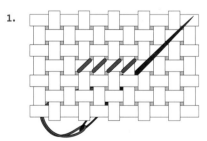

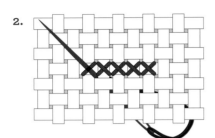

2. Complete each of the half-stitches you just created by moving in the opposite direction, stitching from the bottom right corner to the top left corner of each square. Once you complete the row you're working on, move up to the next row and repeat the method until your color block is completed.

3. When your thread becomes too short to work with easily, simply slip your needle—on the back side of the fabric—under a few stitches (three or four should be fine), pull the floss through, and cut the thread. You'll want to avoid knotting your thread, because it will create bumps that will be visible in your finished piece.

CARRYING THREAD

Most of the time, you'll want to finish a particular color, using the method above, before moving on to a new section. Occasionally, though, you'll want to continue to another section of the same color that is quite close to the one you've just completed. This is called "carrying" the floss, and as long as the sections are no more than four squares apart, it works just fine. Any distance greater than that, and you'll be able to see the floss through the front side of your fabric (especially if you're working on white Aida cloth).

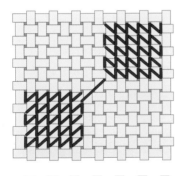

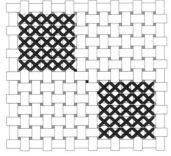

BACKSTITCH

The backstitch is a good friend to turn to when you want to make lines, or add detail to your patterns. To start the backstitch, thread your needle and make two knots in your floss, right on top of each other, leaving a half inch "tail" of floss at the end. Then, find the area where you want your detail line to begin, and, just before that point, push your needle up through the back of the fabric (we'll call this point 1). Your needle should now be on the front side of your fabric. Insert the needle back into the fabric, at the spot where your line should begin (we'll call this point 2). This is your first stitch. To make your next stitch, push your needle up through the back once more, a little ways beyond point 1 (we'll call this point 3). To complete this stitch, come back down through the fabric to close up the gap (we'll call this point 4, though you'll see it's really in the same spot as our original point 1). If you continue with this stitching, you'll keep pushing your needle up through the back of the fabric, a small distance away from the end of your line, and up through the front again to close the line.

In the coming patterns, backstitch is used for all line detail, as well as to outline eyebrows.

SATIN STITCH

Satin stitch is typically an embroidery technique, but in the coming patterns, we'll be using it to fill in the eyebrows of our leading ladies. You'll want to begin by outlining the eyebrows using the backstitch technique you just learned (see left). Then, to fill in the brows, you'll employ the satin stitch.

Start at one end of the eyebrow and push your needle up through the back of the fabric—just inside your outline—and into the fabric just below the top of the outline. Then, push the needle up through the back of the fabric at the bottom of the outline—next to the previous stitch—and back down through the top of the outline. Repeat this process until the eyebrows are completely filled in.

Note: For both backstitch and satin stitch, you do not need to go through the pre-set holes in the Aida cloth. In fact, it's more important to ensure that you're precise with your lines, in order to create the details you want in the finished piece. You may even want to use embroidery needles for these stitches, as you may find that tapestry needles are too dull.

Patterns:
THE WOMEN

CLEOPATRA

◇◇◇ (69 BC–30 BC) ◇◇◇

PHARAOH, TACTICIAN, ENIGMA

CLEOPATRA was Egypt's last active pharaoh. While she is without a doubt one of history's most recognizable women, she is also one of its most mysterious. Her only likenesses can be found on old coins, and the 200-year-old details of her life are shrouded in mystery. Just who was the real Cleopatra? As with so many women of the ancient world, it depends largely on who's telling her story.

Across the many different versions of Cleopatra the one thing that remains consistent is just how much power she had as a female ruler. During her rule, Cleopatra formed smart alliances and had affairs with other powerful leaders. She joined forces with Julius Caesar and aligned with the Romans to oust her brother from the Egyptian throne. Following Caesar's death, she fell in love and aligned herself with Marc Antony, just as Roman civil war broke out. The consummate ruler, she fought for her country until its end.

While the debate continues over whether Cleopatra was truly beautiful, much more was known about her considerable intelligence. Cleopatra declared herself a goddess to unite her people, made Egypt richer while guiding it through turmoil, and fought to keep her homeland independent of the expanding Roman Empire. She was also a well-educated strategist who spoke several languages. While many accounts of Cleopatra paint her as a beautiful seductress, what likely made her much more of a threat to the official writers of history was just how clever a political ruler she was.

To quote the comparatively less-biased Plutarch, the earliest known historian to document Cleopatra's life (doing so around one hundred years after her death):

"For it was not because her beauty in itself was so striking that it stunned the onlooker, but the inescapable impression produced by daily contact with her: the attractiveness in the persuasiveness of her talk, and the character that surrounded her conversation was stimulating. It was a pleasure to hear the sound of her voice, and she tuned her tongue like a many-stringed instrument expertly to whatever language she chose."

Cleopatra and Mark Antony's lives came to a tragic end as Octavian's Roman army encroached upon the couple's combined forces. Mark Antony fell on his own sword after hearing of Cleopatra's alleged death, while she committed suicide by snakebite. Or at least that's the story according to Shakespeare.

These stories about Cleopatra—the woman, the myth, the legend—continue to this day, proving that she remains as powerful a force as ever.

FEMINIST ICON CROSS-STITCH

QUEEN ELIZABETH I

◇◇◇ (1533–1603) ◇◇◇

MONARCH,
LEADER,
MAVERICK

"**I KNOW** I have the body of a weak and feeble woman, but I have the heart and stomach of a king, and a king of England, too," Queen Elizabeth I famously said while rallying English troops in 1588. The Spanish Armada was coming for England, and Good Queen Bess was not having it. In one of the country's greatest military victories, the Royal Navy made the Spanish ships turn around. In her forty-four years on the throne, Elizabeth oversaw the "golden age"—now known as the Elizabethan era—that brought the theater to London and English ships around the globe.

Before a span of British history was named after her, Elizabeth Tudor was born into chaos. The daughter of King Henry VIII and his second wife Anne Boleyn, she was a disappointment to her father who had wanted a son. Henry had Elizabeth's mother beheaded when his daughter was two. He married again soon after, and his male heir, Prince Edward, was born. The nine-year-old Edward became king as England fell into economic and social unrest. When Edward died in 1553, his choice for succession was his cousin, Lady Jane Grey, ignoring Henry's wishes that put Mary, his older half sister, and Elizabeth next in line. Lady Jane was ousted after nine days, and Mary took the throne, determined to make Protestant England Catholic again. Mary executed hundreds of Protestants following a rebellion and jailed Protestant Elizabeth in the Tower of London for her suspected involvement. Little did Elizabeth know that the crown would soon be hers.

At twenty-five, Elizabeth inherited a broken England following Mary's death. During her long reign, she turned the country into the strong and independent nation that it has remained—and she did it by herself. Never married despite Parliament's insisting otherwise, Elizabeth brought Protestantism back while remaining relatively tolerant of everyone's beliefs, protected her country against outside invasion, and provided the stability that allowed for a cultural revolution. As a national identity developed around Shakespeare and the theater, Elizabeth looked outward to expand her empire. Five years after Sir Francis Drake sailed around the world in 1580, Sir Walter Raleigh set up a small colony on the east coast of North America. He called the land Virginia after England's "Virgin Queen."

The beloved queen was married to England, which she had united and strengthened, until her death in 1603.

QUEEN
ELIZABETH I

QUEEN
ELIZABETH I

ABIGAIL ADAMS

(1744–1818)

ADVISER,
FIRST LADY,
PATRIOT

I **N 1776,** Abigail Adams famously urged her husband and his pals in the Continental Congress to "remember the ladies" in drafting a "new code of laws" for the soon-to-be United States of America. In her letter to John, some of the earliest known writing to call for women's rights in America, she warned, "If particular care and attention is not paid to the ladies, we are determined to foment a rebellion, and will not hold ourselves bound by any laws in which we have no voice or representation."

John responded with a letter, teasing her for being "so saucy" and reassuring her of the masculine system's working just fine. While these were radical times—America fighting for its independence from Great Britain—the idea that women should have rights was just a little too revolutionary for the eighteenth century. But that was Abigail in a nutshell. Through speaking her mind and advocating for women's issues at a time when ladies stayed silent, Abigail was a "feminist" long before the term was coined.

Abigail believed that women should have access to education and be valued for their intellect. While she had no formal education herself, she was taught to read and write at home and spent her early years devouring her family's library. Through her own learning, she found that women could serve in much more useful roles if they had the opportunity for education. They could advise on important matters in and outside of the home, manage property, and provide useful perspective.

John saw Abigail as his intellectual equal and constantly asked for her advice on political matters during the Revolutionary period and his later time in the White House. Throughout their lives, Abigail and John wrote more than 1,100 letters to each other. While they didn't always agree on everything, John respected Abigail's opinion and let it be heard. Long before women were even given the right to vote, Abigail was sitting in on debates in the House of Representatives and helping her husband make political decisions about the future of the country.

While the Founding Fathers may not have had "the ladies" in mind when they were drafting the Constitution, Abigail's early call for women's rights would never be forgotten.

Color key:
- 754
- 938
- 355
- 3782
- 762
- 550
- Blanc
- 310

ABIGAIL ADAMS

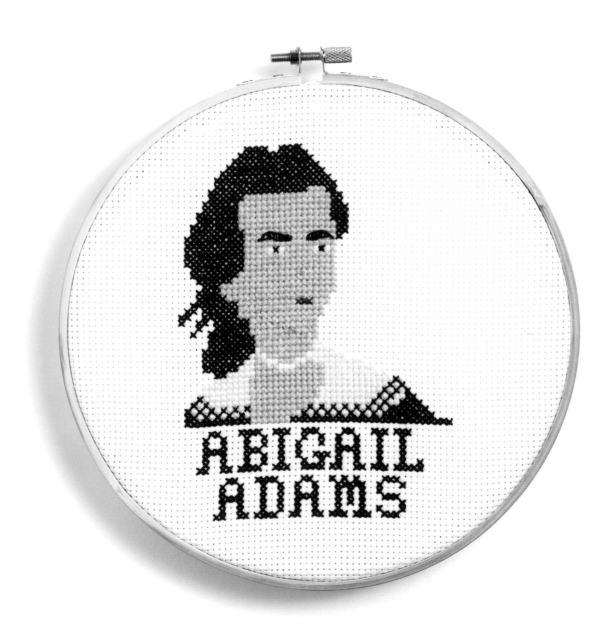

SOJOURNER TRUTH

◇◇◇ (1797–1883) ◇◇◇

ABOLITIONIST, CIVIL RIGHTS ADVOCATE, SURVIVOR

SOJOURNER TRUTH named herself. After hearing what she said was the voice of God in 1843, she left her slave name behind and set off on a new mission as a crusader for civil and women's rights. She spent the following years traveling across America and "testifying the hope that was in her." This hope was that society would one day bring slavery to an end and grant all people, regardless of race, gender, or class, equal rights. Through preaching about what was right, Sojourner Truth helped plant the seeds for the revolutions to come.

Truth was born into slavery as Isabella Baumfree in 1797. In the first third of her life in New York, she was bought and sold several times. Her owners beat her, harassed her, and forced her to do strenuous labor. As a teen, she fell in love with another slave and started a family. While a law had been passed that should have set her free when she turned twenty-five, Truth was still in waiting at twenty-nine. She took matters into her own hands and escaped to freedom with her infant daughter. She later successfully sued for the return of her five-year-old son, making her the first black woman to win a court case against a white man.

A freed slave, Sojourner Truth hit the road to give speeches across the United States on the need for equality. She delivered her most famous speech, which came to be known as "Ain't I a Woman?", at a women's rights conference in 1851. The only woman allowed to speak, she fought against the idea that women were the "weaker sex" and said that men shouldn't be afraid of equality for all people.

Sojourner Truth moved to Michigan in the 1850s, where she helped slaves escape to freedom on the Underground Railroad. During the Civil War, she went to many of the states to recruit black men to fight for the Union army. After the war was over, she headed to Washington, DC and thanked Abraham Lincoln for helping to bring about an end to slavery. In her time spent in DC, she also worked to desegregate streetcars and improve conditions for recently freed slaves.

Through her work "testifying," Sojourner Truth brought revolutionary ideas to the masses. The abolitionist Harriet Beecher Stowe once said of Truth that she couldn't recall meeting "anyone who had more of that silent and subtle power which we call personal presence."

FEMINIST ICON CROSS-STITCH

SOJOURNER TRUTH

SUSAN B. ANTHONY

◇◇◇ (1820–1906) ◇◇◇

SUFFRAGETTE, ORGANIZER, REFORMER

SUSAN B. ANTHONY was a rebel, arrested for voting in the 1872 election.

A born activist for social justice, her Quaker family was committed to social reform, encouraged women's education, and worked to end slavery. Their New York farm became a meeting place for radical thinkers interested in making the United States a more equal place.

Susan continued to keep her family's values in mind when she became a teacher at twenty-six. With this job came the duty of bringing equality to education and the workplace. She encouraged more women to enter the field as teachers and advocated for equal access to education regardless of gender or race. An early proponent of equal pay, Susan encouraged working women to organize.

After she met fellow activist Elizabeth Cady Stanton in 1851, the two became lifelong partners in the fight for women's rights. Both women were active in the antislavery and temperance movements. They formed the National Loyal League in support of the 13th Amendment, which abolished slavery in 1865. They also founded the Women's State Temperance Society and petitioned to limit the sale of liquor in New York. When the government wouldn't accept their petition because it was signed by mostly women, it was clear that women needed the right to vote to be heard at all.

The women's rights movement took off with the two ladies at the forefront—Susan traveling, organizing, and lecturing and Elizabeth writing and giving women a voice to rally behind. They began publishing the radical newspaper *The Revolution* in 1868, which lobbied for women's rights under the motto "Men, their rights and nothing more; women, their rights and nothing less."

They formed the National Woman Suffrage Association in 1869, which pushed for an amendment granting women the right to vote. Seeing it as their human right, Susan and others showed up to vote in the 1872 presidential election and were arrested for it. When she brought her case to the Supreme Court and lost, more women began paying attention. Susan, Elizabeth, and others began writing the *History of Woman Suffrage*, and Susan helped unite all early suffragettes under one group, the National American Woman Suffrage Association, in 1890.

Susan continued gathering signatures in support of voting rights for women, lobbying yearly before Congress. She died fourteen years before seeing the fruits of her labor as women were granted the right to vote in 1920.

FEMINIST ICON CROSS-STITCH

SUSAN B.
ANTHONY

MARIE CURIE

◇◇◇ (1867–1934) ◇◇◇

SCIENTIST,
NOBEL PRIZE WINNER,
INNOVATOR

AT A TIME when science was a man's world, the brilliant Marie Curie was blazing a trail. Madame Curie was the first woman to win a Nobel Prize, the only woman to win a Nobel Prize twice, and the only person to win a Nobel Prize in two different sciences—physics and chemistry. Her work revolutionized science and reminded the world that women deserved a place in it.

Marie Curie was born Maria Skłodowska in Warsaw to two teachers in 1867. The Polish city was under the rule of the Russian Empire at the time, which had done away with lab instruction in schools. This did not faze Marie. She thrived in her classes and learned what scientific training she could from her father, a math and physics teacher.

A top student at a time when women were not allowed at the University of Warsaw, Marie would not be deterred. She and her older sister began taking secret classes for women held at a "floating university." The pro-education rebels that they were, the sisters then made a pact to "get out of Dodge" and support each other at real universities outside of Poland. After Marie worked to send her sister to medical school, she was off to Paris to study at the Sorbonne. This was where she would meet her husband and lifelong collaborator Pierre Curie.

Together, the couple did pioneering research on "radioactivity," a term Marie coined. Their observations of a mysterious glow on uranium salts led to the discovery that energy was being produced from the uranium atom itself. Atomic physics was born as they continued to explore and break down other radioactive materials. In doing so, they discovered two new elements—polonium, named after Marie's home, and radium. A few years after the couple took home their first Nobel Prize in physics, Pierre was accidentally killed by a horse-drawn wagon.

While Marie was heartbroken, she took over Pierre's teaching position and became the first female professor at the Sorbonne. She continued their research into radiation as she saw its potential as a cancer treatment. Marie later went on to work with X-rays during World War I. She assembled a unit of portable X-ray machines that were used on battlefields and ended up preventing suffering in many soldiers' lives.

Marie spent her entire life working on the cutting edge of research, and it was her work with radioactive materials that ultimately took her life. A science martyr in her own right, Marie lived by the words she one wrote in a letter home from the Sorbonne, "One never notices what had been done; one can only see what remains to be done."

FEMINIST ICON CROSS-STITCH

MARIE
CURIE

VIRGINIA WOOLF

◇◇◇ (1882–1941) ◇◇◇

WRITER,
PUBLISHER,
VISIONARY

A WOMAN must have money and a room of her own if she is to write fiction," penned Virginia Woolf in the 1929 book-length essay *A Room of One's Own*. Regarded as one of the twentieth century's most important authors, Virginia was familiar with the limitations that women faced. If women were to find creative success and fulfillment, they'd need the same access to opportunities and a space to think men had.

While her brothers received a formal education at Cambridge, Virginia learned what she could at home in her family's extensive library. Still, her childhood was not an easy one. The sudden deaths of her mother and half sister in 1895 and 1897 led to the first of several nervous breakdowns. When her father died in 1904, Virginia had another episode that left her institutionalized.

These early hardships still did not hold Virginia back from her passion for learning. Between 1897 and 1901, she took courses in Greek, Latin, German, and history at the Ladies' Department of King's College. Here, she came in contact with women interested in higher education reform. Years later, Virginia became involved in an inner circle of writers, critics, artists, and intellectuals known as the Bloomsbury Group. This was where she met the essayist and her future husband Leonard Woolf, with whom she'd open the Hogarth Press.

Virginia Woolf published her first novel *The Voyage Out*, in 1915. Then came many more novels and essays of important literary significance. These included the classics *Mrs. Dalloway*, *To the Lighthouse*, and *Orlando,* as well as the pioneering feminist works *A Room of One's Own* and *Three Guineas*. Virginia's writing was revolutionary at the time for both its style, which was innovative and broke literary norms, and content, which made readers think deeper about issues of feminism, sexuality, class, politics, and discrimination.

Despite her success and love for writing, Virginia sank into a deep depression one last time in 1941. She put on her overcoat, filled her pockets with stones, and drowned herself in the River Ouse. While her life came to a tragic end, her soul lives in the works of others, inspired by what her brilliant mind was able to accomplish when given a space to think.

VIRGINIA WOOLF

FEMINIST ICON CROSS-STITCH

ELEANOR ROOSEVELT

◇◇◇ (1884–1962) ◇◇◇

FIRST LADY, DIPLOMAT, FREETHINKER

ELEANOR ROOSEVELT was more than first lady of the United States. She was a politician, writer, diplomat, and advocate for the rights of those in the minority. For her work in the United Nations on the Universal Declaration of Human Rights, President Harry Truman called her first lady of the world.

Eleanor had grown up an awkward loner in New York. Following the deaths of her parents, she was raised by a critical grandmother who constantly attacked her for how she looked. While her self-esteem was shaken, she got her groove back after being sent to a boarding school in London as a teen. She returned to New York a confident and freethinking woman ready to take on the country's problems. She began volunteering at settlement houses in New York's slums and joined the National Consumers League, interested in improving working conditions for the poor. After she caught the attention of Franklin Delano Roosevelt, they married in 1905 despite her mother-in-law's disapproval.

The couple had six children in the eleven years that followed, and Franklin began working as a politician. When he was struck with polio and rendered unable to walk in 1921, Eleanor often served as his stand-in. New to the political world, she began making appearances and meeting with other leaders in his place. Her political involvement continued when her husband entered the White House in 1933.

Eleanor transformed the role of first lady by taking an active interest in the country's politics and staying outspoken on the issues she cared about. She continually worked to protect and support those who didn't always have a seat at the table—women, African Americans, the working class, and children. She held ladies-only press conferences at the White House at a time when first ladies didn't hold press conferences and women journalists weren't welcome. She ignored segregation laws, responded regularly to the letters she received, and wrote about her views and everyday life in the newspaper column "My Day."

Not your average first lady, Eleanor was the only woman appointed in the United Nations delegation following her long tenure at the White House. She helped draft and promote the Universal Declaration of Human Rights after World War II, which boldly declared that all human beings in the world have certain inherent rights. Described as a modern-day "Magna Carta for humanity," it still remains the world's most translated document.

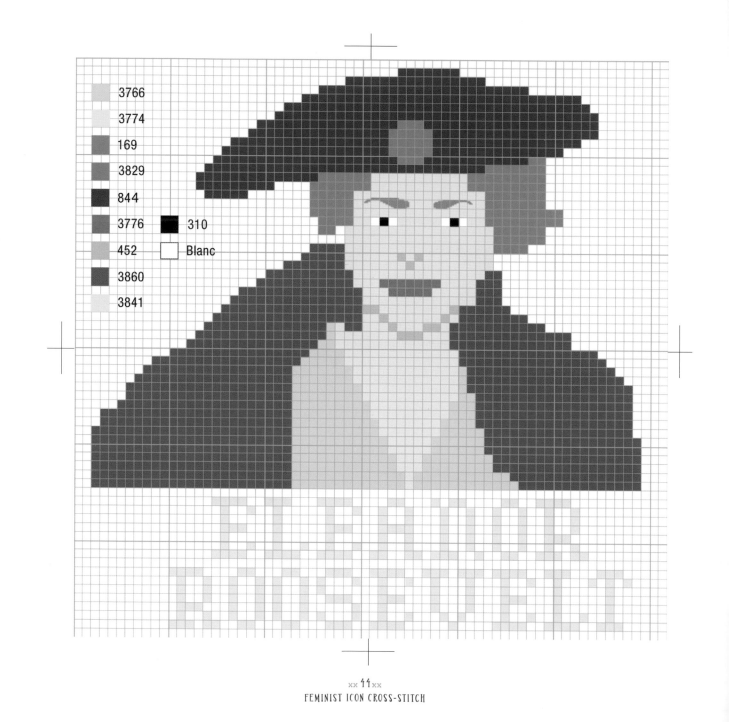

AMELIA EARHART

◇◇◇ (1897–1937?) ◇◇◇

AVIATOR,
PUBLIC SPEAKER,
TRAILBLAZER

AMELIA EARHART was introduced to her first plane as a young woman at a flying expo. She and a girlfriend were standing by themselves in an open field when a stunt pilot dove his plane down at them. "I am sure he said to himself, 'Watch me make them scamper,'" Amelia recalled. Her friend ran off, while she stood her ground. "I did not understand it at the time, but I believe that little red airplane said something to me as it swished by."

That conversation stayed with her for the rest of her life. After taking her first ride in an airplane, by 1920 she knew that her future lay in aviation. She tirelessly juggled a number of jobs—ranging from photographer to truck driver—to save for flying lessons. Then came her first plane, the yellow *Canary*. Only the sixteenth woman licensed to fly, Amelia quickly became both an aviation pioneer and a symbol of female empowerment.

Amelia had always been an independent spirit. Born in Kansas, her family was on the move throughout her childhood from Kansas to Iowa to Minnesota to Illinois. She was raised mainly by her mom, who did not believe in molding Amelia and her sisters into "nice little girls." The girls explored their various neighborhoods, hunting, sledding, and climbing trees. Young Amelia kept a scrapbook of newspaper clippings about successful women working in film, engineering, the law, and other jobs that were typically reserved for men.

Little did Amelia Earhart know that she would one day be making her own headlines. As an aviator, she took her plane higher than any women had ever gone. In 1932, she flew by herself across the Atlantic Ocean, making her the first woman to ever do so. In 1935, she took on another ocean, becoming the first person to fly across the Pacific from Hawaii to California.

On land, Amelia was also making strides for women. She helped found the Ninety-Nines, an organization for women pilots. When she married publisher George Putnam, she kept her maiden name. Amelia lectured across the United States and wrote about aviation to help inspire other women to enter the field. She was a member of the National Women's Party and an early advocate for the Equal Rights Amendment.

Amelia Earhart took on her life's final challenge in 1937. She became the first to attempt an around-the-world flight and made it most of the way around the globe before vanishing with 7,000 miles left to go. While the mystery surrounding her disappearance continues, her memory reminds women everywhere that the sky's literally the limit.

FRIDA KAHLO

◇◇◇ (1907–1954) ◇◇◇

ARTIST,
INTELLECTUAL,
PROVOCATEUR

FRIDA KAHLO rocked a unibrow with pride. She saw no need to change her masculine features, once writing in her diary, "of my face, I like my eyebrows and eyes." The Mexican painter broke norms in how she chose to live her life and the vibrant art that she created. Frida was weird, honest, independent, and always unapologetically herself.

Frida was a rebellious spirit long before she picked up a paintbrush. She claimed that she was born in 1910, the same year that the Mexican Revolution broke out. She boxed and wrestled to stay active after contracting polio as a young girl. In a family portrait, she proudly wore a suit as a teen. One of the few female students accepted at the elite National Preparatory School in 1922, she joined a gang of politically minded leftist intellectuals. When she was traveling on a bus with the gang's leader and her then lover in 1925, a trolley car struck the bus and a steel handrail impaled Frida through the hip.

Frida Kahlo started to paint during her long and painful recovery, creating the first in a long line of self-portraits. These portraits were honest and emphasized Frida's faint mustache as much as the colorful flowers that she liked to wear in her hair. She connected with famous Mexican muralist Diego Rivera to see what he thought of her work. The two became romantically involved in 1928 and married soon after. They had separate but adjoining houses and studios, and both had affairs. Frida was openly bisexual and had affairs with men and women. Frida's turbulent marriage and ongoing health problems caused her great suffering that she took to the canvas. Unlike any art that came before it, her paintings were gruesomely beautiful and often focused on the experiences that women silently went through: birth, miscarriage, heartbreak, pain. While some call her art surrealist, Frida later said she just painting her "own reality."

Frida Kahlo continues to inspire new generations of creative women to embrace their inner weird. As she once wrote in her diary, "I used to think I was the strangest person in the world, but then I thought there are so many people in the world, there must be someone just like me who feels bizarre and flawed in the same ways I do. I would imagine her, and imagine that she must be out there thinking of me, too. Well, I hope that if you are out there and read this and know that, yes, it's true I'm here, and I'm just as strange as you."

Color key:
- 834
- 3733
- 3731
- 913
- 3843
- 797
- 445
- 973
- 814
- 938
- 552
- 550
- 783
- 371
- 310
- Blanc

FRIDA KAHLO

FEMINIST ICON CROSS-STITCH

SIMONE DE BEAUVOIR

◇◇◇ (1908–1986) ◇◇◇

PHILOSOPHER,
AUTHOR,
THINKER

"**O**NE IS NOT BORN**, but rather becomes, a woman," the French philosopher and theorist Simone de Beauvoir famously declared in her 1949 book *The Second Sex*.

In her existentialist exploration of what it meant to be a woman, she proposed that women were defined as second to men—and largely, by men. Women became women by conforming to other people's expectations and assumptions. Through exposing that they were oppressed, Simone showed women that they didn't have to look or act a certain way because it was expected. They could rise above.

This idea was so radical that the Vatican put *The Second Sex* on its banned books list. The book had given the world a new way to think about gender and social hierarchies, paving the way for the second-wave feminist movement to come. Women soon realized that they had the power to assert themselves against a patriarchy that had tried to keep them powerless.

Simone had been an existentialist her whole life. Deeply religious as a child, she wanted to become a nun until she had a crisis of faith at fourteen. She continued to ponder the world that she existed in while studying philosophy and mathematics at the university level. As women had only recently been allowed a higher education, she became the ninth woman to ever receive a degree from the Sorbonne. During this time, Simone also began what would be a lifelong open relationship with the existentialist philosopher Jean-Paul Sartre. This union was unconventional to say the least, if not downright scandalous. They never married or lived together, and both were free to pursue other people and sometimes did so together.

Throughout her career, Simone de Beauvoir wrote novels, essays, biographies, and autobiographical pieces about often taboo topics that got people asking deeper questions about society and their role in it. *The Second Sex* remains by far her most influential work. While the feminist thinker would not refer to herself as a "feminist" until the 1970s, her crisis around what it meant to be a woman laid the foundation for the revolution to come.

FEMINIST ICON CROSS-STITCH

PATTERNS: THE WOMEN

BETTY FRIEDAN

◇◇◇ (1921–2006) ◇◇◇

AUTHOR, ACTIVIST, SECOND WAVE PIONEER

BETTY FRIEDAN showed American housewives that they could be happy outside of the home. Her 1963 book, *The Feminine Mystique*, was one of the most influential books of the twentieth century and helped spark second-wave feminism. The book showed women, especially those with comfortable lives in suburbia, that personal fulfillment was something worth fighting for.

In 1921, Betty was born to Russian Jewish immigrants in Illinois. She was a bright student and graduated summa cum laude from Smith College in 1942. While she received a fellowship to train as a psychologist at the University of California, Berkeley, she left after a year to work as a journalist in New York City. In 1947, she married Carl Friedan, and the couple had their first child a year later. Betty returned to work afterwards, but she lost her job after she got pregnant a second time.

While she took on some freelance writing on the side, career-minded Betty was largely unhappy with her new gig as a stay-at-home mom. She wanted more, and when she surveyed her female Smith classmates at a fifteen-year reunion, she found out that they did too. Betty began doing research in history, psychology, sociology, and economics to explain why they all felt so unhappy, what she called "the problem that had no name." The result was *The Feminine Mystique*. The book caught the attention of women across the nation who felt the same, and a social revolution was born.

The overwhelming response led Betty Friedan to cofound the National Organization for Women in 1966. With an army of women behind her, she continued to work on expanding women's rights and helped lead the National Women's Political Caucus in 1971. As one of the women's movement's most powerful leaders, her activist work was influential in helping change laws that were unfair to women. Employers began to improve hiring practices, provide maternity leave, and rethink unequal pay.

Betty showed American housewives that there was much more to life than being married with children. They had potential.

FEMINIST ICON CROSS-STITCH

BETTY
FRIEDAN

RUTH BADER GINSBURG

◇◇◇ (1933–) ◇◇◇

LAWYER,
SUPREME COURT JUSTICE,
DISSENTER

RUTH BADER GINSBURG is known as "the Notorious RBG" for good reason. The Supreme Court justice, now in her early eighties, is no stranger to dissent. She even wears a black and gold collar when she feels like justice has been wronged. The small powerhouse has spoken out against inequality and unfairness throughout her entire career— and on the Supreme Court bench since 1993. Ruth has shown young girls and women alike that disagreeing with what's established is not only okay, but key to social progress.

Ruth has been defying the norm since she was one of nine women in a class of about 500 at Harvard Law School in 1956. The dean at the time reportedly questioned her and the other female students upon their arrival, "How do you justify taking a spot from a qualified man?"

Ruth graduated at the top of her law class, finishing her degree at Columbia after moving to New York for her husband's job. As a woman and mother, it was difficult for Ruth to find employment in a male-run legal world. When she did become a professor at Rutgers in 1963, she was told that she'd make less than a man because she had a husband with a good job. A victim of discrimination, Ruth was inspired to rectify the inequalities that she faced early on.

The first tenured woman at Columbia Law School in 1972, Ruth cofounded the first law journal that focused on women's issues, cowrote the first casebook on gender discrimination, and cofounded the Women's Rights Project at the ACLU. She went on to argue six gender discrimination cases before the Supreme Court between 1973 and 1976. She won five, changing outdated laws that treated men and women differently. While the Equal Rights Amendment fell short of approval in 1982, Ruth showed legislators case by case that they could no longer write laws that outwardly didn't treat women as equals.

Ruth Bader Ginsburg was appointed a justice on the US Court of Appeals for the DC Circuit in 1980 and to the Supreme Court in 1993. In her life on the bench, her dissents have helped fuel social progress. Congress even passed a law making it easier for women to file equal-pay lawsuits following one of her fiery dissents in the Lilly Ledbetter case. After the law was passed, Ruth said in an interview that this helped changed the game by "giving women the courage to demand what they are entitled to."

Through being notorious in her disagreements, Ruth has shown women that they are entitled to equality.

PATTERNS: THE WOMEN

GLORIA STEINEM

◇◇◇ (1934–) ◇◇◇

JOURNALIST,
FEMINIST,
REBEL

GLORIA STEINEM isn't crazy about being called an "icon." For her, the fight for women's rights and equality has always been more about the mission. While the progress made in the women's liberation movement was the result of many individuals working together, Gloria helped give women a voice. It was her trailblazing work as a writer and feminist activist in the 1960s and '70s that made the need for change more apparent.

Gloria got her start in journalism as a freelancer in the early 1960s, a time when newswriting remained an old boys' club. In between assignments on food and fashion, she took on pieces that brought women's issues to the forefront. In 1962, she wrote about the unfair choice women have to make between career and marriage after being told by *Esquire* to rework a piece about contraception. The next year she famously went undercover as a Playboy Bunny and exposed how poorly treated these women were on the job.

By 1968, she was a founding editor at *New York* magazine and worked as a political columnist. Her article "After Black Power, Women's Liberation" made national news as a call to arms for women everywhere. Then along came *Ms.* in 1972, the first national magazine that was controlled exclusively by women. The magazine, cofounded by Gloria, focused on social and political topics that few were talking about out in the open. The first issue of the magazine sold out in a week.

Gloria's activism went hand in hand with her writing. She actively campaigned for the Equal Rights Amendment, designed to guarantee equal rights to women. In 1971, she joined other feminists to form the National Women's Political Caucus and stated in a speech: "This is no simple reform. It really is a revolution. Sex and race, because they are easy and visible differences, have been the primary ways of organizing human beings into superior and inferior groups and into the cheap labor on which this system still depends. We are talking about a society in which there will be no roles other than those chosen or those earned. We are really talking about humanism."

Gloria Steinem is still fighting the good fight for equality around the globe today. She continues to work as a political activist and feminist organizer, traveling around the world to talk about issues of equality in different cultures. Her voice has helped give women a louder one.

FEMINIST ICON CROSS-STITCH

ROSIE THE RIVETER

◇◇◇ (WWII) ◇◇◇

WORKER, POSTER GIRL, SYMBOL

EVERYONE KNOWS ROSIE. She's that lady in the blue jumpsuit and red bandanna with the "We Can Do It" attitude. Or maybe she's remembered best for her cover of the *Saturday Evening Post* during World War II. On it, she's pictured on her lunch break with a riveting gun on her lap and her foot on top of Adolf Hitler's *Mein Kampf*. Hardworking Rosie even inspired a top radio hit around the same time. As the song goes:

All the day long whether rain or shine
She's a part of the assembly line
She's making history
Working for victory
Rosie the Riveter

But who was this Rosie? She got her start as a fictional character, a tool used by the US government to encourage women to enter the workforce. Over time, she grew into something much bigger—a powerful symbol of women's economic power. This was due, in large part, to the millions of real-life Rosies she came to symbolize during World War II.

With men at war and national morale high, women took over the positions that were left behind. And these Rosies weren't just putting rivets into aircraft carriers. They were welding ship parts together, repairing airplanes, serving as radio operators, and even doing the work that led to the atomic bomb. Because of the important labor of so many women at home, victory soon became possible abroad.

When the war ended, many of these jobs were returned to the men that once held them. Still, the workforce would never be the same. These units of Rosies had shown the world and themselves that they were capable of anything if given the opportunity. This ultimately expanded the type of work available to women in the United States. Not only that, it showed women that there was much more out there for them.

While there's still work to be done in the workplace in terms of equal rights and pay, Rosie the Riveter serves as a reminder that progress is possible. With the right amount of muscle, women can do anything.

BILLIE JEAN KING

◇◇◇ (1943–) ◇◇◇

ATHLETE,
EQUAL RIGHTS ADVOCATE,
CHAMPION

BILLIE JEAN KING ruled both on and off the court. The American tennis great was ranked number one in the world for five years and took home thirty-nine Grand Slam singles, doubles, and mixed-doubles titles in her career. Off the court, she fought for equal prize payouts for women and was one of the first well-known openly gay athletes. Billie Jean famously said that she "wanted to use sports for social change," and her life is proof of just that.

Growing up in Long Beach, California, Billie Jean raised money to buy her first racquet after her parents told her she should ditch softball and football for a more "ladylike" sport. A born athlete, she stuck with it. In 1961, she became a part of the youngest team ever to win a Wimbledon doubles championship at seventeen years old. The titles kept on coming as Billie Jean fought her way to the top. She won her first major singles championship at Wimbledon by 1966 and officially went pro in 1968.

Billie Jean became the first female athlete to earn over $100,000 in 1971, but pay inequalities still existed with women getting less prize money for wins. Billie Jean organized other female players and founded the Women's Tennis Association. They threatened to boycott the US Open in 1973 if equal prize money was not offered to all athletes. The Open responded and became the first major tournament to offer equal payouts for men and women.

That same year, Billie Jean captured the nation's attention when she beat former tennis star and self-proclaimed male chauvinist Bobby Riggs in 1973's "Battle of the Sexes." She showed the close to fifty million tuned in that women were not inferior to men and would not fold under pressure. The win showed the world that there was nothing wrong with being a female athlete and helped turn on a new audience to Billie Jean's favorite sport.

Billie Jean King went on to become one of the first women to ever coach professional male athletes in the World Team Tennis, a mixed-gender professional league. Elton John even wrote a song in honor of the team she was a player-coach for, the Philadelphia Freedoms. She came out about her sexuality in 1981. While this lost her some endorsements at the time, she gained a new group of fans in the LGBT community for her strength, and she continues to advocate for them today.

One of the greatest athletes to ever knock around a tennis ball, Billie Jean King used the power that came with her skills to level the playing field for all athletes.

FEMINIST ICON CROSS-STITCH

BILLIE JEAN KING

HILLARY RODHAM CLINTON

◇◇◇ (1947–) ◇◇◇

SECRETARY OF STATE, PRESIDENTIAL CANDIDATE, BOUNDARY BREAKER

HILLARY RODHAM CLINTON is a "nasty woman." In the final debate of the 2016 US presidential election campaign, Hillary transformed a petty insult into a feminist rally cry. To be a nasty woman, she demonstrated, was to be intelligent, ambitious, and prepared for the job. It was to be outspoken and keep your cool in the face of interruption. The first female major-party presidential candidate ever, hardworking Hill showed women not to doubt themselves. To be powerful was to be nasty.

Long before her run for president of the United States, Hillary Rodham was student government president at Wellesley College. A social justice activist, she was the first student ever nominated to speak at Wellesley's commencement in 1969. Yale Law School followed, where Hillary was one of twenty-seven women in a graduating class of 235. She met Bill Clinton and developed an interest in children's rights.

Hillary and Bill Clinton moved to Arkansas and got married in 1975. Bill became the state's governor, while Hillary taught criminal justice and worked as a lawyer, becoming the first ever female partner at her firm. Fighting for education and health care, Hillary put her community first as first lady of Arkansas. Still, she was not always well received by it and even publicly criticized for keeping her maiden name and continuing to pursue a career outside of being Bill's wife. She tacked on "Clinton" to the end of her name after being blamed for Bill's loss in the governor's race in 1980. This still did not slow her down. In 1988 and 1991, she was named by the *National Law Journal* as one of the top 100 lawyers in America.

From first lady of Arkansas to first lady of the United States, Hillary was never typical. When Bill was elected president in 1992, Hillary took an active role despite warnings by the administration that it might make Bill appear weak. As a first lady, Hillary used her voice to help people, especially women, who couldn't always speak up. In 1995, at the United Nations Fourth World Conference on Women in Beijing, she boldly proclaimed to the delegates from 180 countries that, "Women's rights are human rights, and human rights are women's rights." Women deserve the same protections and opportunities as everybody else.

Throughout the rest of her career, Hillary would continue to fight for equality and justice as a US senator from New York and Barack Obama's secretary of state. No stranger to criticism, especially about how she should or shouldn't act as a female leader, Hillary always kept her cool. She showed strong, nasty women of all ages just how far their ambition could take them.

FEMINIST ICON CROSS-STITCH

PATTERNS: THE WOMEN

MICHELLE OBAMA

◇◇◇ (1964–) ◇◇◇

PUBLIC SERVANT,
FIRST LADY,
ROLE MODEL

"**T**HIS COUNTRY BELONGS to you," Michelle Obama reminded young Americans in her final speech as first lady of the United States. "Do not ever let anyone make you feel like you don't matter or like you don't have a place in our American story, because you do. And you have a right to be exactly who you are."

Long before warm and insightful Michelle became the first African American first lady in the White House or a proud mom, she was a young girl growing up on the South Side of Chicago. Raised in a working-class family, she was educated at Princeton. The privileged Ivy League often made her feel like an outsider, but it did not faze her. Harvard Law School was next. While working toward her degree, she also worked to show the university the value of enrolling students and hiring professors that looked more like her. As a lawyer at a top law firm in Chicago, she met her husband and future president of the United States, Barack, and was assigned to be his mentor.

Michelle soon knew that her true passion was in public service. She worked as assistant to the mayor and then assistant commissioner of planning and development in her hometown of Chicago. Then it was on to becoming executive director at Public Allies, a nonprofit that prepares young people for public service. In 1996, Michelle started the first community service program at the University of Chicago as the associate dean of student services. She continued to give back while working at the University of Chicago Hospitals, becoming their vice president for community and external affairs in 2005.

In her eight years as first lady of the United States, Michelle continued to work toward improving her community by advocating for poverty awareness, healthy living, and improved education for young girls around the globe. She invited young students from all different backgrounds through the White House's doors and charmed America as they watched her dance and sing karaoke on late-night TV. While she was always coming off as kindhearted and carefree, she's also been frank and not afraid to speak out on injustice and inequality—calling out hate when she sees it and reminding people of all ages not to let the haters get them down.

Perhaps the president said it best when he thanked Michelle in his farewell address, "You made the White House a place that belongs to everybody. And a new generation sets its sights higher because it has you as a role model. You've made me proud. You've made the country proud."

BEYONCÉ

◇◇◇ (1981–) ◇◇◇

PERFORMER,
ARTIST,
ICON

WHEN QUEEN BEY stood in the dark, silhouetted by the word "FEMINIST" glowing in giant letters, it was hard to look away. Beyoncé brought feminism to the masses with her performance at the 2014 MTV Video Music Awards. And once the "F" word was on display in living rooms across America, it got people talking. What did it mean to be a feminist? And just who did that word belong to? Through her anthems of female empowerment and actions as the queen of the pop kingdom, the all-powerful Beyoncé has shown a larger audience of women that they could be sexually empowered and a feminist at the same time. They could be whoever they wanted to be and still believe in basic equality.

From her career in the girl group Destiny's Child to her breakout as a solo artist, Beyoncé has worked to empower independent women, survivors, single ladies, and girls destined to run the world. Her music, which is often self-reflective, and personal experiences have shown women that while the female experience is complex, it's also what unites us. Women can maintain their personal freedom and want a family, strive to keep their partners happy and be as successful as them, and use their privilege to stand up for those who may not have a platform. Women could be sexy and sexually empowered. Women can be self-reliant and slay.

Beyoncé's power doesn't just come from her celebrity. It's comes from how she's used her platform. When she performed at the 2013 Super Bowl, she hired all women from all different backgrounds to sing, dance, and play in her band, the Sugar Mamas. In 2016, an all-female drum line played as women in Black Panther garb got in formation to stand up against police brutality and racial injustice. And Beyoncé's more recent visual album *Lemonade* explores pain and healing through a black woman's experience, and it does so while mixing her music with the words of the Somali-British poet Warsan Shire. In showing women, especially black women, their value, she's inspired college courses on black feminism and female empowerment.

While the word "feminist" may have a complex history, the meaning's quite simple according to Bey, who made the term more inclusive by forcing everyone to stare at it head-on. In her song "Flawless," she drops the following definition by the Nigerian writer Chimamanda Ngozi Adichie over a beat: "Feminist: a person who believes in the social, political, and economic equality of the sexes."

FEMINIST ICON CROSS-STITCH

MALALA YOUSAFZAI

◇◇◇ (1997–) ◇◇◇

NOBEL PRIZE WINNER,
ADVOCATE,
INSPIRATION

MALALA YOUSAFZAI was eleven years old when she took on the Taliban. The group had taken over her hometown in Pakistan. Television and music were banned, places of learning were bombed, and women weren't allowed far from home. Malala just wanted to go to school.

"How dare the Taliban take away my basic right to education?" she bravely asked in a speech at a local press club. Malala talked about hiding her books and spoke out about how the Taliban were preventing girls from going to school. As the military tightened its control, Malala began reporting on the ground for the BBC. Writing under the pen name Gul Makai, she kept an online diary for the world to read about her life as a Pakistani schoolgirl.

When Malala was exposed as the author, this brought her both praise for her strength and threats from the Taliban. In 2011, she was awarded Pakistan's first National Youth Peace Prize and nominated for the International Children's Peace Prize. The next year, she was attacked by a masked gunman while on her school bus. She was shot in the head, neck, and shoulder with a single bullet.

Malala survived and miraculously recovered at a hospital in the UK. In response to the shooting, the world fought back. Protests broke out across Pakistan, petitions were signed by millions, and Pakistan's first Right To Free and Compulsory Education bill was passed. The UN launched a petition calling on all countries to guarantee children the right to an education and outlaw discrimination against girls.

What didn't kill Malala made her stronger. The teenager became a global advocate for all girls, told the world her story in the book, *I Am Malala,* and set up the Malala Fund to raise money to open schools and empower girls to speak up and demand change.

"Some people only ask others to do something. I believe that, why should I wait for someone else? Why don't I take a step and move forward," Malala said in 2013 to a crowd at Harvard University. "When the whole world is silent, even one voice becomes powerful."

Malala's voice and spirit made her the youngest person ever—and the first Pakistani—to win the Nobel Peace Prize in 2014. She put the $500,000 toward creating a secondary school for girls in Pakistan. Today, she continues to fight for peace and education through encouraging world leaders and opening schools for girls across the globe.

MALALA

Patterns:
THE WORDS

FEMINIST ICON CROSS-STITCH

A WOMAN NEEDS A MAN LIKE A FISH NEEDS A BICYCLE

310

892

FEMINIST ICON CROSS-STITCH

PATTERNS: THE WORDS

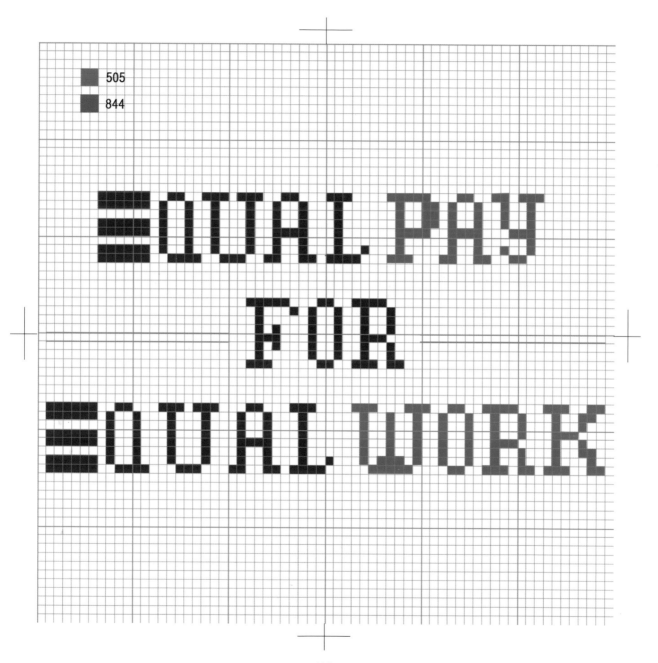

FEMINIST ICON CROSS-STITCH

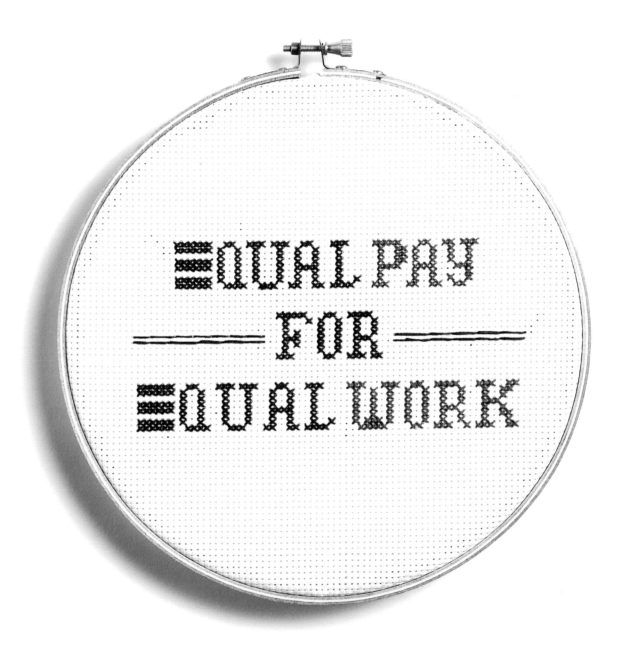

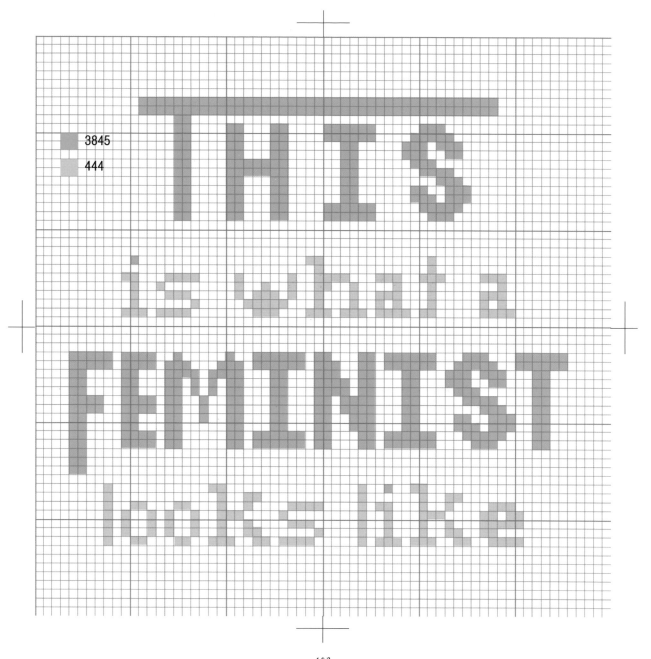

THIS is what a FEMINIST looks like

3845
444

FEMINIST ICON CROSS-STITCH

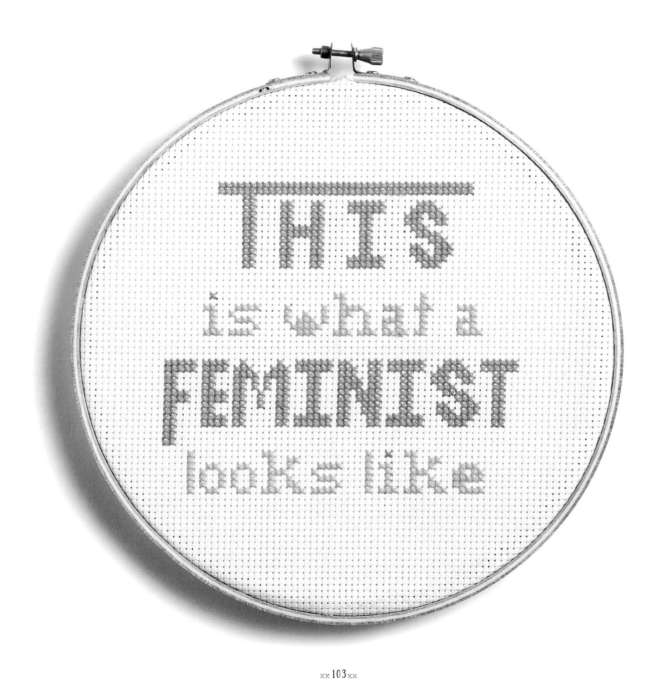

FEMINIST ICON CROSS-STITCH

nevertheless she persisted

Legend:
- 3801
- 3845

FEMINIST ICON CROSS-STITCH

PATTERNS: THE WORDS

FEMINIST ICON CROSS-STITCH

FEMINIST ICON CROSS-STITCH

WOMEN
BELONG
IN THE
HOUSE
AND THE
SENATE

814
921

FEMINIST ICON CROSS-STITCH

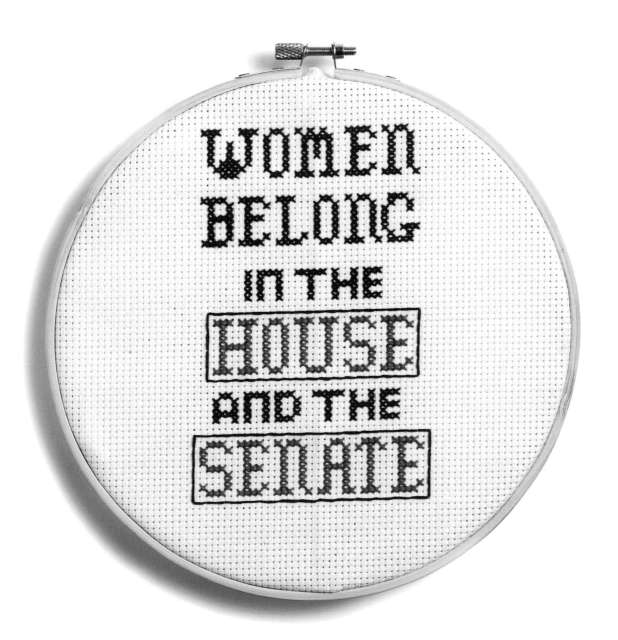

Acknowledgments

If anyone had asked my twelve-year-old self what I'd be doing right now, my very last guess would be this—the book you are currently holding. And there are so many people without whom it wouldn't have been possible.

Thank you to my Mom, for forgetting that she taught me how to stitch, and for fostering my love of all things crafty and obscure.

Thank you to my Dad, for teaching me that an A is never as good as an A+, for keeping the Feds off my back, and for believing that I can do anything that comes my way.

Thank you to Shannon Connors—the best editor and friend a girl could possibly hope for. Your patience, faith, and ability to anticipate made this all possible.

Thank you to my brilliant co-author Lauren Mancuso. Without your words, this would just be a bunch of squares. Thank you for giving my patterns a voice. Thank you to Amanda Richmond—without your flawless vision, taste, and design there would literally not be a book.

Thank you to Liore Klein, for being my constant in this crazy journey. I could not have done it without the only sister I've ever not had. Thank you to Rachel Pologe, for very gently nudging me forward and making sure I was still alive when I disappeared for weeks at a time. Thank you to Alex Acosta, for learning how to cross-stitch purely to help me finish this, and for generally keeping me organized and together. Last, but not least, thank you to Gary Sundt, for weathering all storms with me, for being there for me always, for ten million fried shrimp emojis, and for generally existing.

And finally, to every bad-ass woman who is and isn't in this book, without whom literally nothing is possible.
—ANNA FLEISS

So many amazing women are responsible for this project. Outside of the Glorias, Ruths, and Michelles, there are the Shannons, Emilys, and Donnas. Thank you to Shannon Connors for taking a chance on me as a writer, assembling the perfect team to give every woman's story new life, and being the best editor a girl could ask for. Thank you to Emily Costa for being a lifelong pal and proofreader. I'm a better writer and thinker because of you. And thank you to those who taught me what a strong woman was at a young age—my hardworking and always sassy mother, Donna Mancuso, and the high school teacher who first introduced me to the "f" word (feminism), Donna Ring. I love you both.
—LAUREN MANCUSO

Index

A

Abolitionist, 26–29
Activists, 30–33, 58–59, 66–67, 78–79
Adams, Abigail, 22–25
Anthony, Susan B., 4, 30–33
Artists, 50–53, 86–87
Athlete, 74–75
Authors, 38–40, 54–55, 58–59
Aviator, 46–47

B

Backstitch, 12
Basic cross-stitch, 6–12. See also Cross-stitch
Beauvoir, Simone de, 5, 54–57
Beyoncé, 4, 86–89
Black feminism, 87. See also Feminism

C

Children's rights, 43, 79, 91
Civil rights, 26–27. See also Equal rights
Cleopatra, 14–17
Clinton, Hillary Rodham, 78–81
Cloth/fabric, 6

Cross-stitch
backstitch, 12
basics of, 6–12
carrying thread, 11
cloth for, 6
description of, 6
fabric for, 6
floss for, 7
history of, 4
hoop for, 7
introduction to, 4–5
multiple cross-stitches, 10–11
needles for, 7
samplers, 4
satin stitch, 12
scissors, 7
single cross-stitches, 9–10
stitches for, 7–12
techniques for, 7–12
thread for, 7, 11
tools for, 6–7
women patterns, 13–93
words patterns, 95–115
Curie, Marie, 4–5, 34–37

D

Discrimination, 5, 39, 55, 63, 75, 91

Dissenter, 5, 62–63

E

Earhart, Amelia, 46–49

Economic equality, 87

Economic power, 71

Education reform, 4, 38–39

Education rights, 5, 23, 31, 78–79, 83, 91

Elizabeth I, Queen, 4, 18–21

Embroidery floss, 7

Embroidery hoops, 7

Embroidery scissors, 7

Empowerment, 4–5, 47, 71, 87, 91

Equal rights, 4–5, 38–41, 47, 54–55, 63,
    66–75, 82–83, 87. See also Women's rights

Equality, 23, 27, 31, 59, 63, 67, 75, 79, 83, 87

F

Fabric, 6

Female empowerment, 4–5, 47, 71, 87, 91

Female leaders, 15, 18–19, 43, 59, 79

Female presidential candidate, 78–79

Female ruler, 14–15

Feminism, 39, 59, 87

Feminist movement, 55, 59, 66–67

Feminist sayings, 95–115

Feminists, 4–5, 23, 39, 66–67, 86–87

First Lady, 22–23, 42–43, 78–79, 82–83

Floss, 7

Floss, carrying, 11

Friedan, Betty, 58–61

G

Gender discrimination, 5, 55, 63, 75

Ginsburg, Ruth Bader, 5, 62–65

H

Health care rights, 78–79

Hoops, 7

I

Intellectuals, 5, 23, 39, 50–51

J

Journalists, 43, 58–59, 66–67

K

Kahlo, Frida, 50–53

King, Billie Jean, 5, 74–77

L

Lawyers, 5, 62–63, 78–79, 83
Leaders, 15, 18–19, 43, 59, 79

M

Multiple cross-stitches, 10–11

N

Needles, 7
Nobel Prize winners, 5, 34–35, 90–91

O

Obama, Michelle, 82–85
Oppression, 5, 55

P

Patterns
Abigail Adams, 24–25
Amelia Earhart, 48–49
Betty Friedan, 60–61
Beyoncé, 88–89
Billie Jean King, 76–77
Cleopatra, 16–17
Eleanor Roosevelt, 44–45
Elizabeth I, 20–21
Frida Kahlo, 52–53

Gloria Steinem, 68–69
Hillary Rodham Clinton, 80–81
Malala Yousafzai, 92–93
Marie Curie, 36–37
Michelle Obama, 84–85
Rosie the Riveter, 72–73
Ruth Bader Ginsburg, 64–65
Simone de Beauvoir, 56–57
Sojourner Truth, 28–29
Susan B. Anthony, 32–33
Virginia Woolf, 40–41
women patterns, 13–93
words patterns, 95–115
Performer, 86–87
Philosopher, 54–55
Political role, 42–45
Political ruler, 14–15
Presidential candidate, 78–79
Provocateur, 50–53
Public speaker, 46–47

R

Racial injustice, 87
Rebels, 4–5, 30–31, 66–67
Reformer, 30–31
Role model, 82–83
Roosevelt, Eleanor, 42–45
Rosie the Riveter, 70–73

S

Samplers, 4. See also Cross-stitch

Satin stitch, 12

Sayings, patterns for, 95–115

Scientist, 5, 34–35

Scissors, 7

Single cross-stitches, 9–10

Social justice, 30–31, 55, 78–79

Social reform, 30–31

Social revolution, 59

Steinem, Gloria, 5, 66–69

Stitches, 7–12. See also Cross-stitch

Suffragettes, 4, 30–31

Supreme Court justice, 62–63

Symbolism, 70–71

T

Techniques, 7–12

Theorist, 54–55

Thread, 7

Thread, carrying, 11

Tools, 6–7

Truth, Sojourner, 26–29

V

Voting rights, 4, 30–31

W

Women, defining, 4

Women, patterns of, 13–93

Women, sayings for, 95–115

Women's movement, 55, 59, 66–67

Women's rights, 4–5, 23, 27, 30–31, 47, 59, 63, 66–67, 78–79. See also Equal rights

Woolf, Virginia, 38–41

Words, patterns for, 95–115

Writers, 38–45, 54–55, 58–59, 66–67

Y

Yousafzai, Malala, 5, 90–93

BOSS *Babe*

EQUAL PAY
FOR
EQUAL WORK

THE
FUTURE
IS
FEMALE

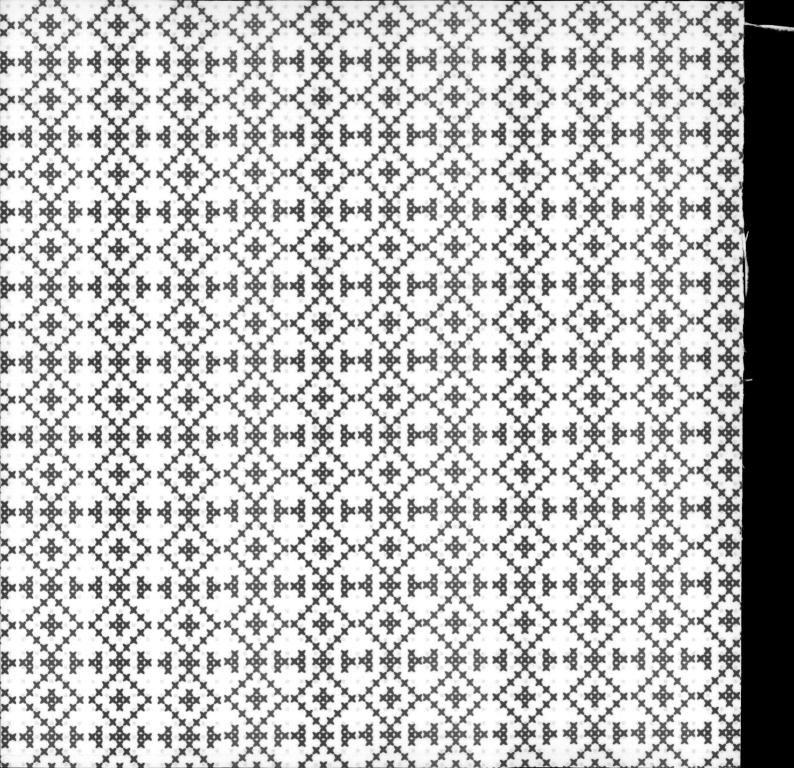